# Tiny Paw Prints, Touching Tails

## Stories of Devotion, Tenderness & Healing
### *for Those Who Love Cats*

Inspired by Faith

Tiny Paw Prints, Touching Tails
©Product Concept Mfg., Inc.

Tiny Paw Prints, Touching Tails
ISBN 978-0-9886719-9-7
Published by Product Concept Mfg., Inc.
2175 N. Academy Circle #200, Colorado Springs, CO 80909

©2013 Product Concept Mfg., Inc.  All rights reserved.

Written and Compiled by Cynthia Musick
in association with Product Concept Mfg., Inc.

All scripture quotations are from the King James version
of the Bible unless otherwise noted.

Scriptures taken from the Holy Bible,
New International Version®, NIV®.
Copyright © 1973, 1978, 1984 by Biblica, Inc.™
Used by permission of Zondervan.
All rights reserved worldwide.
www.zondervan.com

Sayings not having a credit listed are contributed by writers
for Product Concept Mfg., Inc. or in a rare case,
the author is unknown.

# Tiny Paw prints, Touching Tails

*Always I have a chair for you in the*
  *smallest parlor in the world, to wit, my heart.*

Emily Dickinson

Cats—everything about them is charming and delightful, at least to a cat lover. Often discriminating, sometimes demanding, but always devoted, cats offer their unlimited unconditional love.

The stories in *Tiny Paw Prints, Touching Tails* are from people who share their lives and their laps with cats. It's a celebration of the many ways cats impact our lives with their curious, comforting, and playful ways. Our feline friends have a special place in the world. Cats show up when they are needed and impart lessons only they can teach. These furry companions treasure and enjoy each day, reminding us to live mindfully in the present moment.

What's more comforting than a kitty curled up contentedly on your lap? The sweet purring presence of a cat has calming, healing powers. Natural-born comedians, cats can also entertain and distract even the most stressed human companion.

*Life is just better with a cat.*

# The Healing Power of "Purrrr"

Hit and run. The car sped down the street as the badly injured black and white kitten summoned the strength to pull herself to the curb. She was dragging the right side of her tiny body when a kind passer-by gathered up the frightened, injured little ball of fur and took her to the animal shelter.

There they tried to save both legs, but ended up amputating the front right one. Fortunately, Allison was at the shelter that day. She and her husband Isaac are both intensive-care nurses who foster cats and often choose those with medical issues. Allison gladly took home her tiniest patient to tend until the stitches came out.

They named her "Mittens" because of the white markings on her remaining three legs. As the days passed, Mittens began to trust Allison and Isaac as they cared for her wound, administered antibiotics, and loved her back to health. By the time Mittens was strong enough to return to the shelter, they'd fallen in love with her and there was no turning back.

Now they've made their apartment handicap-accessible by strategically placing small boxes so Mittens can jump more easily onto window sills or their bed. Having only three legs doesn't seem to trouble Mittens. What she may lack in agility, she makes up for in her sweet temperament.

When the couple comes home from long shifts at the hospital, Mittens happily hobbles out to greet them, like a little bouncing tripod. The stressful day of two critical-care nurses melts away when Isaac scoops up Mittens and cradles her, as Allison strokes her soft fur. Adorable little Mittens always purrs as loudly as she can.

Mittens' "purr therapy" helps the couple to heal from work days filled with emergencies, trauma or loss. It's amazing how the unconditional love of a tiny kitten can make such a big difference.

# A New Cat-egory of Talent

When the Musick family adopted their first cat, they decided to name him Mozart because he's one of their favorite composers—plus they thought "Mozart Musick" had a melodic ring to it. They had originally wanted a small shorthair cat, but when they visited Purr-fect Adoptions, they fell in love with the orange striped, long hair Maine Coon mix. With his flowing mane and dignified appearance, he probably should have been called Beethoven.

Mozart fit perfectly in the musical family. If the lid of the grand piano was open, he'd catch a nap or two inside it. When the two daughters practiced their violins, he would jump up and bat at their moving bows.

Eventually, he'd fall asleep in their velvet-lined violin cases, purring rhythmically like a furry metronome as they played Bach, Beethoven, and of course, Mozart. It was his way of encouraging them to practice and enjoy classical music.

Mozart also worked as the family's cat receptionist. Callers found it hard to believe when he'd answer the landline phone—a skill he somehow taught himself. After he raced to the ringing phone, he'd bat at the receiver until he had it in his huge paws, toss it back and forth like a pizza crust and finally drop it. He'd then lick the receiver, letting loose with a loud "Purrrrrrrrr…"

The parents may have accidentally encouraged Mozart's phone skills when their daughters were much younger. While away at camp or staying with friends, the girls would call and ask to put Mozart on the phone. He'd hear their voices and start purring, licking the receiver as if he thought the sweet children who played with him were actually hiding inside the device.

At first it appeared that Mozart just liked the challenge of getting the phone off the hook and pressing the keys, so they let him play with an old, disconnected model.

But this merely permitted Mozart to perfect his craft, and soon he was getting to ringing phones before they were. The entire family would race around the house yelling, "Mozart—we've got it! Don't pick up!" Of course, he ignored them.

If neither feline nor human reached the ringing phone in time, Mozart would cock his head and listen patiently to the message being left on the answering machine. Then he'd take his huge paw and push the annoying, blinking "erase" button.

Perhaps it was jealousy that motivated Mozart to make his first phone call. An adorable black kitten named Lucky had just joined the family. Mozart had never asked for a brother. Maybe he was trying to reach the pet store to send his little sibling rival Lucky back where he belonged.

For whatever reason, Mozart decided to take matters into his own paws and pressed down on that nice big key on the kitchen desk phone—the one set to automatically dial 911. Yes, instead of the pet store, Mozart dialed 911.

Two police officers soon showed up at the door to investigate a strange emergency call that involved what sounded like purring. Thankfully, they hadn't ordered an ambulance yet. The Musicks apologized and vowed to keep their "children" from playing with the phones.

Now that everyone in their family has cell phones, they aren't as much at the mercy of Mozart's answering service. But lately, they have noticed their black cat Lucky playing on the computer keys. And of course on the Internet, no one knows you're a cat.

## Feline Physical Therapist

Jordan and Jackson, both gray tabby kittens, arrived in time for Christmas. But it soon became apparent that Jordan had a problem.

Four-year-old Alex told his mother that Jordan didn't walk the same way Jackson did. Lauren, busy mother of two, examined the kitten. From her training as a physical therapist, she realized the kitten had an injured hip. So she loaded Alex and the small kitten into the car and rushed to the vet's office.

There the doctor repaired the kitten's hip, and Jordan was able to return home. For a couple weeks, Lauren needed to sequester Jordan so he could heal properly. During this time, Lauren did physical therapy with the kitten, moving his hind leg in different positions. She made it a combination play time—physical therapy session for the cat, who sometimes even purred as they did the exercises. Lauren found this to be a calming time for her as well.

Now Jordan races around the house with ease. The cat was Lauren's tiniest patient...one who paid her in purrs.

ANYONE
NEEDING
CPR...
CAT
PURRING
RESUSCITATION?

# Rudy the Cat Burglar

He looked like a bandit, with black and white markings forming a mask on his furry feline face. Rudy stole the hearts of Dorothy and her daughter Kaitlin when they first saw him at the animal shelter. Little did they know what else he would steal.

Rudy loved living with his new family and was allowed to come and go as he pleased. But his happy life almost ended when Rudy was struck by a car. Dorothy rushed him to the vet and spared no expense to repair his internal injuries.

Fortunately, Rudy healed nicely from his accident and was as lovable as ever, but some of his behavior changed dramatically. He began leaving home every night and bringing back socks and then pantyhose. He did this for several nights, and then expanded his felonious feline habits. Over time he brought home oil filters, boots, coin purses, ice scrapers, t-shirts, a baseball glove, a size 14 sneaker and even a doll. His "robbery range" was two to three blocks in all directions from his home.

One night Rudy jumped from a neighbor's tree to their second-floor roof, got in their little boy's open window and stole not one, but both of his slippers.

Rudy must have carried them home one at a time, which meant he had to re-trace his steps up the tree, over to the roof, in the window and back down. All this was done in the middle of the night while the boy was in bed. Surprisingly, the boy didn't wake up.

One morning, 17 pairs of work gloves appeared on Dorothy's lawn. The neighbors on the corner were having extensive repairs done on their house. The workmen had left a lot of their tools and equipment on the neighbor's porch to save them time in the morning. The 17 pairs of gloves all came home over the same night, which meant Rudy had made 34 trips to the neighbor's porch and back.

Dorothy and her family finally concluded that Rudy was showing his gratitude, paying them back for saving his life by bringing them all these stolen gifts. By now, the whole neighborhood knew Rudy the cat burglar.

Dorothy asked her neighbors to contact her first if they were missing anything. So she would regularly get calls from people asking her to look through Rudy's stash for specific missing items. The people next door once called and asked if Rudy had brought over airline tickets because they couldn't find them (but no, Rudy was more into cloth than paper).

The cat's kleptomania actually seemed to bring the neighborhood closer together. Dorothy and her family really got to know their neighbors. Fortunately, they were all good-natured about it and didn't seem to mind. "We now know the shoe size of everyone on the block," commented Dorothy.

Their subdivision had a yearly 4th of July parade—a small, child-focused one. So annually, Dorothy's family would lay out all of Rudy's stolen booty and paraders would pause to look at and pick up their possessions before marching on.

Rudy became legendary. The local city newspaper picked up his story as did a national women's magazine. He also was part of a radio spot with an animal psychologist.

All of this led to Rudy and Dorothy being flown to New York City for an appearance on a late-night talk show. Minutes before going on air, Dorothy discovered the theme for the evening's program was "Real Oddities."

But Rudy was not an "oddity," he was a grateful and resourceful cat. His cat burglaries brought neighbors together, provided good-natured humor, and gave Dorothy a whole new set of friends. Rudy had stolen their hearts…along with just about everything else in the neighborhood.

## Pepper to the Rescue

Pepper always added spice to Amy's and Chris's lives. They adopted the black Maine Coon, along with her sister Merlot, and brother Roux. All three cats were smart, but Pepper was a true genius. She would learn how to do something, then teach her cat siblings so they could all get into trouble.

One day Amy was working in her kitchen when Pepper stood almost dog-like as a pointer–pointing to the dishwasher. Pepper insisted that Amy open the dishwasher. And when she did, she found Merlot trapped inside it.

Pepper was the most fastidious of the three cats and didn't like any sort of smelly mess. Once Chris found his sock in the middle of the room and when he picked it up, discovered that Pepper had used it to cover a mess.

Pepper's dislike of anything foul-smelling would eventually be an incredible blessing. One of the first spring days, the couple opened up their screened-in porch for the cats to enjoy the day, while they went out for lunch.

When Amy and Chris returned, Pepper was on the screened-in porch, standing on the back of an Adirondack chair, screaming and howling as if to say, "Something is wrong!"

Amy walked over to the outside corner of the screened-in porch to calm down Pepper, but immediately smelled the odor of gas. Amy called the gas company, who arrived quickly and confirmed the leak. Something had gone wrong in moving the meter from the basement to outside, the day before.

Once inside the house, the couple would probably never have smelled the gas. Amy and Chris were so grateful that Pepper had alerted them. Pepper was more than a cat—she was a lifesaver.

# A Lucky Mess

Browsing at the local pet store is entertaining, but it's risky to do on the weekend of Adopt-a-Pet. Who can resist all those cute cats begging to be adopted!

Cynthia's daughters pleaded with her to stop at the pet store, only so they could hold the new kittens. They were already "servants" to one cat at home, so she thought they were safe from the temptations of adorable baby kittens.

When her younger daughter Melissa held the jet black kitten with soft, sleek hair, he licked her hand. The note on the front of the crate read: "Bud was rescued as a dog was chasing him down the street." Melissa remarked, "Oh he's so lucky that someone saved him!" She and her sister Allison continued stroking his fur as he let out a little squeak of a meow. The next thing they knew, they were adopting and taking home "Lucky."

The new little feline had to be kept in Melissa's room and gradually introduced to their other cat, Mozart. Lucky soon became part of the family and now has his own ritual. Whenever a family member sits down, he jumps on an available lap and stretches out as though the human is his personal chaise lounge.

Lucky feels it's his mission to help the family decompress after a difficult day. So when David, Cynthia's husband, collapses into the recliner after work, Lucky is right there. He leaps onto his lap, then climbs on top of his chest to neutralize the stress of the day, administering CPR…Cat Purring Resuscitation.

This cat also has a sharp eye for design. When Melissa was in eighth grade, she spread out her science project all over the dining room table. On the official science project board, a foam-core triptych, she laid out her research paper, lettering, and some graphs showing the results of her experiments.

Evidently, Lucky did not agree with her scientific conclusions. He threw up on her project board. Melissa thought her project was ruined. She was upset, but not with Lucky. Mainly, she was frustrated with herself for letting him out of the basement while she was assembling the project.

Fortunately, Melissa managed to salvage the science project by adding some eye-catching cut-outs and redoing the graphs where Lucky had made the mess.

Fast forward to the Science Fair. Melissa ended up winning the grand prize trophy. When she arrived home, she had her picture taken with Lucky and the trophy. She was convinced the changes Lucky had "suggested" helped her to win. Melissa recognized that from a crisis can come a blessing, and that a little mess can be a Lucky thing.

NEVER GET TIRED
OF BEING AWESOME.

## Angel Kitty

A quilt pattern of cats adorns their bedspread and photos of cats decorate their walls. These "cat people," Beverly and Martin, have opened their homes and hearts to felines most of their 60 years of married life. So when their cat Ben, a grayish Maine Coon, was going on 20 years, family and friends worried about the time when Ben's ninth life would end.

Concerns disappeared when one day a tiny stray kitten appeared on Beverly's and Martin's doorstep. They fed her, eventually taking her in, and calling her "Little Kitty." Strangely, the more she grew, the more she began to take on the appearance and actions of Ben.

A few months later, Ben passed away and Beverly and Martin felt God had sent Little Kitty as a gift from Heaven to help them through their grief, so she became "Angel Kitty."

Angel Kitty was a special companion to Martin–digging in the garden when he was weeding it, snoozing next to him for an afternoon nap, even lying on her back and waving her paws while Martin did his back exercises!

When hospitalized for a hip replacement, Martin missed Angel Kitty as much as she missed him. From the hospital, his daughter drove Martin to the rehab center, but "detoured" first to his house. She fetched Angel Kitty, who began to shriek with joy when she saw Martin. In the car she sat on his lap, sweetly purring as he stroked her fur and talked to her.

Martin faced weeks of painful rehab but he was motivated to walk again because he knew Angel Kitty needed him. Besides, who would do back exercises with her?

# Spooky Lessons

Everything "cat" was new to Cathy when she brought home a beautiful black Himalayan. Cathy knew she had a lot to learn about cat care, but she really had no idea just how much this little feline was going to teach her about life in general.

*Lesson #1:* Know thyself... or at least thy cat. They'd been home for less than an hour when she became alarmed by an odd sound coming from the kitten's chest. Cathy immediately thought her new kitten was ill with some sort of respiratory disease. She rushed him to the Animal Clinic where the vet examined the kitten and told Cathy the "respiratory illness" was called "purring."

*Lesson #2:* Enlist help, especially from children. Cathy had never named a cat before, so as a teacher she enlisted the help of her third graders. She held up the kitty's picture and heard comments like, "How about Blackie? He looks sort of Spooky." So the class voted and Spook was the winning name.

*Lesson #3:* Trust your instincts and those of your cat. Spook tutored Cathy in the feline ways and tried to influence her social life. Cathy was dating a couple of guys at the same time: Steve, a confirmed dog person, and Mike, a guy who didn't really like dogs or cats. Spook sensed this and always squeezed himself between Cathy and Mike on the sofa, to send the message, "She's really not available, at least not to you!"

Cathy also noticed that when Steve came over, Spook was much friendlier. Over time, Steve's kind and loving heart won over Spook and Cathy, so she chose him over Mike. And after they were married, Steve became a "cat person," too.

*Lesson #4:* Be resourceful or beware of those who are. Together the couple moved to a new home where Spook had a good view of the outside world from the screen door on their front door. A little neighbor girl, Sandi, would often come over to play with Spook, who enjoyed the antics of this sweet kindergartner.

One day when she was there, tossing a small ball for Spook, Sandi proudly boasted that Spook came to visit her every night. Cathy said that she must be thinking of another kitty since Spook was strictly a house cat.

But one night when she couldn't find Spook anywhere in the house, she looked outside, thinking he may have somehow slipped out the door. The porch light was on at Sandi's house and Cathy could see the little girl on the front porch, petting Spook. Now this was, well, spooky! How could Spook have escaped?

Cathy waited until Sandi went into the house and her parents shut off the porch light. Since Spook was a black cat, Cathy couldn't really see him as he scurried home in the darkness, but as soon as he reached their screen door, she saw him deftly push in the screen and slip inside. Once inside, he bent the screen back in place and made it look intact and undamaged.

Over the years, Spook taught Cathy many valuable lessons about life and about cats. She laughs when recalling how she thought purring was a respiratory disease when she first adopted Spook.

Her very first cat had done such a great job of training Cathy that now she and Steve have expanded their family to include three cats. And her feline trio continues the educating and tutoring first established by a little black cat named Spook.

# The Fantastic Feline

Felines are truly fantastic creatures. Boldly authentic, cats let you know upfront their moods and what's on their minds, ignoring you in disapproval or purring with praise. We humans can fake a smile or pretend to like someone. But if people could purr like cats do...now, that would be a genuine barometer of emotions.

Fastidious and self-assured, felines have no need for jewelry, tattoos or piercings to enhance their beautiful coats. Cats have their own sense of style. Although some people mistakenly describe cats as being aloof, it's actually called confidence.

Our furry companions usually behave in ways that showcase their elegant movements. The great tightrope walkers have nothing on the agile cat. The sure-footed felines saunter gracefully across rods of a clothes rack or along tops of fences. An old French proverb captures it best, "The dog may be wonderful prose, but only the cat is poetry."

We humans could take a cue from our cats by remaining true to our inner feelings and renewing ourselves with an occasional nap in the sun.

# WHAT GREATER GIFT
## THAN THE LOVE OF A CAT?

CHARLES DICKENS

## Love Overcomes All

Love conquers all—so the adage goes. And sometimes small creatures can remind us of this important truth. Such was the case with Allison and her feisty cat Taffy.

Allison had grown up with two family felines, so when she went off to nursing school, she knew that her apartment wouldn't be a real home without a cat.

Walking down the cat row at Animal Haven to choose her new kitten, Allison heard a mournful mewing, a pleading cry that translated into, "Please choose me—please take me home!" Allison looked over to see a tiny orange tabby kitten…and her heart melted. The kitten had chosen her.

But before leaving the shelter with her newly-adopted feline, Allison was warned that this kitten had been taken away from her mother too soon, so there might be behavioral problems.

Allison named her Taffy, since she'd pulled at her heartstrings. This small, sweet kitten didn't look difficult; she thought the shelter workers must be mistaken. Tiny Taffy fit perfectly in the pocket of Allison's hospital scrubs.

But as the days passed, Taffy seemed overly aggressive—scratching and biting Allison when she'd try to hold or pet her. When Allison would walk across the room, Taffy came out of nowhere with a Ninja attack, nipping at her legs. The vet counseled her to squirt water at Taffy, but instead Allison mainly just kept loving, loving, loving her.

When she wasn't busy clawing the furniture or window blinds, Taffy was shredding Allison's clothing. How could such an adorable kitten be so rough? Allison joked that Taffy must have been in a "cat gang" before being adopted because she seemed so ruthlessly tough.

But Allison, a caring student nurse, continued nurturing and loving Taffy, buying cat toys for her, and studying at home instead of the medical library so Taffy would not be alone so much. These were all little things, but all done with great affection.

When she'd get home from classes, she'd call out, "Taffy, cuddles!" And that was the signal for the two of them to snuggle up in a big comfy chair and just have some together time…which slowly became longer and longer.

Taffy was smart. She learned if she pressed a certain button on Allison's bedside clock, then that big, nasty sound wouldn't blare out and send her human away.

After Allison slept through several early morning classes, she tried to shut Taffy out of her bedroom so the alarm would not be turned off. Of course, Taffy just cried pitifully at the bedroom door, and Allison ended up letting her back in the bedroom—and buying a new alarm clock.

Fast forward a couple of years. Taffy, although still somewhat of a cat diva, is totally devoted to Allison. She cries when Allison puts on her scrubs in preparation for leaving for her job at the hospital. Whenever Allison is packing for an out-of-town trip, Taffy hisses at the suitcase. Or if the suitcase happens to be open, the cat jumps inside.

Eventually Taffy became a calmer more affectionate cat because she consistently knew nothing but love from Allison. Cats have the right idea: love conquers all. Or at the very least, it will encourage a cat to curl up on your lap.

## Baby Faith

Someone had heartlessly abandoned a mother cat and her entire litter at Nicole's mother's farm in Kansas. Nicole and her husband Mark were visiting for the weekend when they discovered the abandoned treasures in the machine shed.

But the noise and activity of Mark repairing the tractor there must have made Mama Kitty decide to move her brood once again. This time she chose the safe and quiet barn.

The next day Mark was surprised when he heard a mewing sound in the back corner of the machine shop. What should he find but one of the kittens…the beautiful, long-haired Siamese-looking one with blue eyes. When he picked her up though, he was shocked to see that her back legs were mere twig-like extensions folded underneath her. The mother cat had known this kitten was not like the others, and it seemed she'd left it behind to die.

Nicole and Mark, however, had plenty of faith that this baby could survive. They named her Baby Faith and took her back home to Kansas City with them. There they bottle fed her and mostly carried her around. But as the weeks passed, they saw the ingenious cat use her rear end as a makeshift hind leg as she hopped around.

Then they watched in amazement as Baby Faith managed to navigate by walking only on her front legs!

Baby Faith is now healthy and thriving. She is actually bossy to Nicole's and Mark's other cats. She began as an underdog, so to speak, and is now, surprisingly, the matriarch of their cat family. She's also become friends with their Brittany Spaniel and can be seen grooming the dog by licking his face.

Baby Faith has incredibly strong front legs since they are her only support. When she hugs you, you know it! Baby Faith shows such inspiring confidence; she doesn't think of herself as different or handicapped in any way. The small, frail kitten has become a fearless, friendly and loving cat. She may be called Baby Faith, but the faith she has in her own abilities is not small at all.

## *Legacy of Love*

Michelle did not like cats. When she was a kid, she had cat-sat for a neighbor whose cat bit her whenever she'd tried to approach it. Enough of cats; she preferred dogs.

But as an adult, she changed her mind. Michelle worked with Peggy, who was on the board of the local animal shelter and was always urging Michelle to adopt a cat. On one occasion Peggy took her to the shelter, but there Michelle was too overwhelmed by all of the needy animals in one place.

But finally Peggy convinced her. She was fostering a pregnant cat and told Michelle she could have the pick of the litter. Michelle chose the runt and named her Cola, since she was cola-colored.

But Cola had behavioral issues from the beginning. At the time, Michelle was living in a condo with avocado green shag carpeting, which

Cola took to be the Great Outdoors and used as her litter box.

Michelle thought Cola might be acting out because she was lonely. So she moved Cola to the lower level and slept on an old couch beside her to keep her company. She says that may be when they first truly began to bond.

When Michelle married Bob, he brought his own cat, Pico. Although Cola tolerated Pico, she didn't want him to encroach on her territory. Michelle accidentally discovered an advantage in this. If Michelle wanted Cola's attention, she would yell for Pico instead. This would make Cola so jealous she'd come running and meowing to Michelle to complain.

Over time, Michelle came to believe that Cola was her feline soul-mate, and that Cola really loved her. Michelle's rational husband Bob said she was anthropomorphizing and Cola simply loved the fact that Michelle fed her. But even Bob eventually became convinced of Cola's affection.

One day, Michelle was feeling very sick and was lying on the living room couch. Cola came over, sniffed around her mouth, and then proceeded to lie down on Michelle's stomach.

Every day Cola was obsessed with getting her small serving of wet cat food that was dispensed to her and Pico at exactly 5 o'clock. Nothing got in the way of her making a beeline to the kitchen for her share. Sometimes she'd even get there first and eat Pico's serving and hers.

But on this day, when Bob ran the electric can opener to open a can of cat food, Cola looked up, then looked back at Michelle, then back at the can opener, and settled back down on Michelle's tummy to continue comforting her.

Cola was utterly devoted to Michelle for the next 15 years. Toward the end of Cola's life, Michelle and Bob had to give her weekly saline treatments since her kidneys were not functioning well. Michelle was traveling a lot for her job then, and she was wracked with guilt that she couldn't spend more time with Cola.

Michelle recalls one time when she got home from an out-of-town conference and rushed to Cola's little bed, where she had been lying without much movement for days. Cola perked up and even stood up, as if to say "Mom's home… everything's going to be okay."

When Cola passed on, she left behind a legacy of love…and another confirmed cat-lover in this world.

## Old Blue Eyes is Back

Betty was out for her daily walk one day when she heard frantic meows coming from up in a tree. About four feet off the ground, lodged in the fork of a big oak was a frightened Siamese kitten. Betty brought him home, fully intending to find someone else to adopt him, but it was too late. One look into the big blue eyes of the kitten and Betty was smitten.

With his Siamese meows that sounded some-what like singing and his striking blue eyes, the cat earned the name "Frank," after Old Blue Eyes himself, Mr. Frank Sinatra.

Betty grew up during the Big Band era and enjoyed music from that period of time. Strangely, Frank liked to "sing along" to Betty's CDs in his Siamese way, especially when Sinatra crooned the song My Way. When friends came over, Betty played the famous Sinatra song, and Frank entertained them with his vocalizing. Frank the Feline's signature piece became My Way.

I'VE GOT A BIG HUG
    WITH YOUR NAME ON IT.

# *The Cat Who Restored Laughter*

When Sean first met Biscuit, the gray tabby was scampering around the animal shelter, chasing a dog biscuit. Several minutes later, the vet appeared with the same cat perched on his shoulder like a pirate's parrot, and this time the feline appeared to be winking at Sean.

But Biscuit wasn't really winking, although it would be in his personality to do so. He'd been abandoned in a field and brought to the shelter. Both eyes had been infected, but the vet could only save one. He also suffered from abdominal problems, so the vet wanted to continue a treatment of antibiotics and observation. Sean and his wife, Priscilla volunteered weekly at the shelter, so they made a point of playing with Biscuit as he recovered there.

Right before Labor Day, the vet asked if they'd like to take Biscuit to their house, just for the holiday weekend. They already had several pets—dogs and cats, so what's one more cat?

Especially when it's only for a couple of days. Of course, "a couple of days" stretched to forever when they fell in love with Biscuit, who made himself at home right away.

Strangely, Biscuit ignored the other cats in the house, but quickly made friends with their Lab mix Max and their Border Collie mix Shiloh. The cat seemed to think that he was just one of the dogs…a "cog" so to speak.

Biscuit would charge up and down the hallways with Shiloh, sometimes jumping on his back and riding him like a bucking bronco. Biscuit had no fear of smacking Shiloh or Max if they didn't behave, but usually they got along remarkably well. Both dogs had been rescued from adverse situations, so they seemed grateful to have a sweet, new playmate.

Sometimes Biscuit would hide behind the large potted plants, leaping out in a surprise attack when Max wasn't looking. During the day, they'd wrestle like a couple of pups, even though Max was a lanky Lab and Biscuit was a compact cat. At night, Biscuit would sleep snuggled next to Max and Shiloh...just as any other dog might do.

Sean was so grateful for Biscuit. This cat-who-thinks-he's-a-dog and his silly antics brought laughter back to their home. Joy and laughter had been missing for a long time. Sean and Priscilla had endured a year of devastating losses—two cats, one dog, a sweet great-aunt, and Sean's beloved father. The year had been stress-filled and bleak. Now little Biscuit with his energetic personality seemed to brighten and lighten all areas of their lives.

And then, after many hopeful years, Priscilla became pregnant and gave birth to darling twins Liam and Grace. Biscuit loves the babies and especially loves what comes with them—two baby swings and two bouncy seats and a double dose of toys.

If Priscilla is feeding Liam, then Grace is in the swing…and Biscuit is enjoying himself in the second swing. If both the twins are in the swings, then Biscuit entertains himself in one of the bouncy seats. How thoughtful of Mom and Dad to bring a carnival into the living room.

Often Biscuit positions himself between the twins, playing with them and their fascinating toys…always making them giggle. Biscuit is the twins' magical, animated plush toy; they pat his fur and he responds with a loud "Purrrrrr".

Right from the beginning, with his knowing "wink", Biscuit seemed aware of how much love, light and laughter he was going to add to a certain family's life…and they've never stopped being grateful.

## *Man's Best Friend*

John is a great guy who really likes cats but occasionally feels forced to defend his position. He finds that some men count it as a sign of masculinity not to like cats—they'll even adamantly claim to prefer dogs just because it sounds more macho.

Is it because cats seem soft and weak? They're not. True, most cats won't defend you in a fight, but most dogs won't either unless they're trained or bred to do so. But John grew up with a courageous cat named Punchy, a little black and white female, who was certainly the exception.

Once, on John's family's farm in Iowa, a vicious retired police dog named Honcho, who lived up the road, cornered John and a pal against an electrified cattle fence. The dog was snapping and growling as though they were a pair of fleeing criminals.

Suddenly, John's cat Punchy shot out of the ditch, landed on Honcho's back, and delivered several swats to his nose and a bite to the ear.

The terrified dog scooted back up the road, howling and thrashing until Punchy jumped off him. Honcho never returned to John's farm.

For years Punchy accompanied John and his siblings on long hikes into the hills, guarding over him and his black German shepherd, Aris, whom Punchy regarded as one of her offspring.

Years later, when John was serving in the Army, his mother wrote him that Punchy had finally died of old age. "I bawled unashamedly," John admitted. "I still think about that cat."

But it would be several years before cats came back into his life, as part of his wife's household. Now John and his spouse rescue cats and even help feed a feral colony. John believes that his life has been richer and more rewarding because of cats…especially a brave little one named Punchy.

## *Mama Mia*

On one of the hottest days of the summer, Mia received a frantic phone call from her friend Kelly, "Can you help me rescue a trapped kitten? If we don't act fast, he may not survive this heat." Immediately Mia, confirmed cat-lover, was off to lend a hand.

When Mia arrived, Kelly took her to a large wall in the backyard. Wedged between it and another retaining wall was a tiny, crying kitten. They surmised the mother cat had left him there for safety reasons since there were several dogs in the neighborhood.

The heat of the day was relentless and the situation looked impossible. Neither of them could reach the trapped kitten. Then Mia recalled she had a "reacher" device in her car. This long rod-like apparatus enables someone to retrieve objects from a distance. At the end of it are prongs that open and close.

She tied cloth around the prongs to soften them and carefully slid the gadget between the walls, quickly snatching the little guy. Once free, the tiny Maine Coon mix acted dazed.

Mia named him "Wally" because of his dramatic rescue from the walls. He could barely walk; Mia guessed he was only about two weeks old. "Mama Mia" became her new title. As surrogate mother, Mia bottle fed the new baby every two hours. After every feeding, she'd burp Wally and rub him with a warm cloth to replicate what his feline mother would have done to stimulate the kitten's urinary tract.

Since Mia worked full-time, she took Wally to a friend's house during the day so the regular feedings could continue. But every day from five in the afternoon till seven the next morning, Mama Mia was back on duty. She slept next to

Wally on a futon in the sunroom, so he could be isolated from her other two cats. Mia began to get the glazed-over, sleep-deprived look of a new mother, except Mia wasn't allowed any maternity leave to care for this baby. She could barely function at work.

When Wally (finally!) reached four weeks of age, his schedule became more manageable, with Mia able to feed him over her lunch hour. She's the only mother Wally has ever known. She gradually introduced Wally to her other two cats, who also learned to love Wally. And Mia? She now has great respect and admiration for any new mother…human or feline.

A WELL-SPENT DAY
  BRINGS HAPPY SLEEP.
LEONARDO DA VINCI

## "T" is for Tenderhearted

Megan had just graduated from college and moved back to her parents' farm in Missouri while she was job hunting. During her stay there, one of the family's barn cats had a litter of the cutest kittens ever, so she phoned all her friends from college to find homes for them.

Megan's sorority sister Erin came to see the kittens and fell in love with the one with patches of orange, cream, and chocolate brown. She looked liked a tortoiseshell cat, so Erin named her Tortie. Throughout college, Erin and Megan had the habit of calling each other by only the first letter of their names—"Erin" was called "E" and Megan was called "M" so it was only natural to call Tortie "T" for short.

When T came to live with Erin and her new husband Eric, they had only been married a couple of months. Eric wasn't exactly happy to have a cat (being a dog man) but it wasn't long before he was hooked. T was treated like she was their little baby and adored the attention from both Erin and Eric.

After a couple of years, their first child (of the human species) was born and everyone wondered how T would react to Baby Kyle. T was a little standoffish at first—she kept her distance. Perhaps T had hoped this new little creature was just a visitor and that their household would get back to normal. At first, T just watched Baby Kyle, listened and kept to herself.

However, the new little one was not only there to stay, but he'd been showered with lots of toys. Erin made sure that T also received some baby toys, a stuffed bunny and a stuffed doll that looked like a mailman. T almost wore out Erin and Eric with all her playing...hiding her little bunny and mailman, and then finding them again. She coped with the stress of a new baby by focusing on her own playthings.

When Baby Kyle was about three months old, Erin returned to her job part-time and Grandma Kathy became a part-time nanny. Baby Kyle was a good baby but like all babies, he still had a good amount of crying to do.

Grandma Kathy would gently rock her new grandson or walk the halls upstairs and down. She tried just about everything to calm the baby: placing him stomach-down along her forearm, doing a sort of "colic dance" with him, and singing lullabies. Sometimes it worked; sometimes it didn't.

One day, after about 45 minutes of Baby Kyle's constant crying, T came racing down the stairs to the living room where Grandma Kathy was rocking the baby. She noticed that T did not come down alone. In her mouth T had her stuffed bunny that she dropped at Grandma's feet; then ran to get the toy mailman and did the same. Then T looked at grandma, back at the toys, and again at Grandma as if to say, "Here, try these." And it worked! Baby Kyle stopped crying and stared at T and her toys. The baby seemed to relate to the generosity of this cat. Grandma Kathy was relieved and grateful for T's help. From that day on, Baby Kyle was entertained by T's antics, and T accepted the new little guy.

Fast forward 13 years. T is still devoted to Kyle, who is now is a teenager and has two siblings. Kyle is still close to T and now shares his video games with the tenderhearted tortie that fits him to a T.

# A Trio of Blessings

"No, we can't keep this litter of three kittens you've found," Alex said to his disappointed sons Josh and Jonah, ages 6 and 5. "I'll take them to the shelter on Monday. Now please go with your mother to stay at Grandma Miller's for the weekend."

Alex and his young family had recently moved into a beautiful, old Victorian home, built in Virginia about 1890. The wood-frame home had strikingly-tall ceilings and was just the place they'd dreamed of raising a family.

All day Saturday, Alex had to work at his job at the Port Authority, so his wife Becca and sons left to visit her mother.

When he finished his long, 12-hour Saturday shift on the job, Alex didn't have the energy to go upstairs to the bedroom. Instead he fed the kittens, plopped in the recliner, and quickly fell asleep.

But in the middle of night he was awakened by sharp claws on his back and loud mews! The kittens were all over him, and fortunately they were, since Alex now smelled smoke. He grabbed the kittens and ran out of the house to use the neighbor's phone to call the fire department.

Unfortunately, a fire had started in the basement, probably due to old wiring, and had shot up the walls. A house this old did not have smoke detectors or firewalls.

There was extensive damage to the house, the worst in Josh's bedroom. Alex and Becca said a special prayer of thanks that their sons were not home at the time and for the three kittens who had saved Alex.

"We're keeping all three of these kittens," Alex smiled, "they rescued me, so I'm rescuing them!"

## Special Delivery

Midnight was ready to deliver her kittens any day. The two little girls in the household, Laurie and Cynthia, were beyond excited as they thought about the kitties that were about to be born to their very own cat.

Their mother had fixed a large box with blankets in it for Midnight to have as her special birthing place. But Midnight had other ideas.

That bright summer morning Laurie and her sister had played dress-up, trying on their mother's floor-length gowns and clomping around in her high heels. When done playing, they piled the gowns in the corner of their parents' bedroom. Later that afternoon, while they were playing outside, Midnight slipped away to that same bedroom for a quiet and safe spot to have her family.

Midnight must have known she was going to have female kittens since she chose their mother's beautiful, long pink satin gown as her nursery of sorts. On the dress, she gave birth to tiger-like Tigger and the yellowish-orange Cheetah.

But now the beautiful floor-length, pink satin gown was completely ruined. Both of the girls thought they would really be in trouble. Hadn't Mom told them to hang up the gowns in the closet when they were done playing? Strangely, their mom didn't seem to mind, and she let Midnight stay in the bedroom, making certain the new mother was comfortable and well-fed.

Now that they're grown with children of their own, Laurie and Cynthia can look back and understand the unspoken bond of mother-hood between their mom and Midnight. Both mothers knew that the safe arrival of a baby into the world was more important than any satin dress.

# Playing Chicken

One autumn day, a small gray tomcat wandered onto Esther's farm. But he seemed afraid of the cats already living in the barn. Because he was so small, Esther thought her cats may have bullied him. She named the little guy Tom-Tom.

Tiny Tom-Tom was a coward, a scaredy cat, a chicken…until he saw the real chickens! Then he felt right at home with them. And the chickens welcomed the timid kitty.

Now, after several months, it's as if Tom-Tom is just one of the chickens. The chickens have totally accepted their newest BFF, Best Feline Friend. And Tom-Tom thinks of them as his BFF's, Best Feathered Friends.

When Esther calls the chickens to go into the shed at night, Tom-Tom comes, too. He sleeps and eats with them. Esther gives him his cat food in a dish in the chicken shed, and he eats it right alongside the chickens. (The chickens like his cat food too.)

Tom-Tom has the right idea: go where others accept you, try to find the world you like, and create your own "family."

A GENTLE SPIRIT
    CAN CHANGE THE WORLD.

## *Fake It Till You Make It*

One autumn evening, as Sam was locking up his urban machine shop in an old rundown part of town, he heard a faint mewing sound. "Where are you, little buddy?" he kept calling out. Finally a tiny gray and black tabby came limping towards him. Sam cuddled him in his arms and took him to his car, where the kitten nestled on his lap. Together they drove to an all-night convenience store to get cat food and milk.

Once back at his shop, Sam opened the cat food and when the kitten smelled the scent of it, he started purring loudly, doing figure eights around Sam's legs. After the meal, Sam turned a large empty toolbox on its side, wrapped the little orphan in a blanket, and put him in the box for the night.

The next morning when Sam returned to his shop, he expected to find the cat either hiding in the rafters or frantically pacing around. Instead, he was still wrapped in the blanket and lying in the toolbox. Sam named him Einstein, since he thought it was pretty smart of the cat to stay in the warm and safe toolbox.

Sam put him in his coat and drove to his girlfriend's house. There Sam opened his coat, and out spilled Einstein…whose blue eyes and sweet look just melted Paige, so Einstein had a new home.

Paige already had two older cats and a dog. Einstein blended right in and acted like he owned the place. He began to rule the house and the neighborhood. He chased squirrels out of the trees and away from the house.

If another cat wandered into the yard, Einstein would run out and stand there defiantly, staring down the intruder until he left. Occasionally there was a fight, but usually Einstein would puff out his fur to project his powerful little street-smart personality.

Once a Shar-Pei wandered onto their property, and Einstein grabbed the dog's loose skin and started to sway with it! Fortunately, the dog didn't seem to mind, but he did stay clear of Einstein's house after that.

Often when dogs would infringe on Paige's property, Einstein would sit on his haunches and raise both paws. The dogs were so stunned by this bravado that they'd usually leave.

Once that didn't quite work the way he'd planned. Einstein had jumped the fence into the neighbor's yard and was going to greet a new dog there when he realized that the terrier was neither friendly nor afraid. He nipped at Einstein's tail, which sent the startled cat climbing straight up a utility pole! He reached the top and really didn't want to come down.

There Einstein perched, seeming to enjoy surveying his kingdom from this lofty spot. Paige finally got a long ladder and climbed up to rescue Einstein. Once she got close to him, he jumped on her head and rode down the pole as if Paige were his own human elevator.

After that incident, Einstein continued patrolling the neighborhood. Even though he was half the size of many of the dogs, he confidently strutted around. Einstein knew that acting the part is half the battle.

## Thawing the Ice

"The relationship I had with my cat Oolah was the most 'human' I've ever had with a pet," confided Rebecca. "We bickered and irritated each other from time to time, but we also belonged to each other."

The Siamese cat that had been named Shadow had lived with a woman in a trailer park but when she passed away, Rebecca helped out. She adopted Shadow when she was about two years old and changed her name to Oolah, a character from a favorite movie.

Rebecca transported Oolah to her Chicago apartment. For the next three days, she complained so vocally that Rebecca couldn't sleep. Then the cat fell silent. Rebecca would come home from work and call out to her...nothing. She'd look behind the couch, under the bed, everywhere until she finally found her. Once she discovered her beneath a pile of clothes in the laundry basket, glaring back at her as if to say, "Leave me alone".

Eventually, Oolah would lay on Rebecca's feet at night. But if she'd try to pet the kitty, she'd bite Rebecca's toes and run away.

Over a year passed and it seemed like this frustrating feline would never warm up to Rebecca. Finally, one spring Oolah's icy emotions thawed with the Chicago snow. Rebecca went on a spring break trip and left her cat for the first time.

When she returned home, she never heard such screaming! Her kitty was so happy that she meowed herself hoarse and purred all over Rebecca. Oolah now appeared to love Rebecca— and not just a little bit, but desperately. Perhaps she also realized that Rebecca had not left her permanently, like her first human had.

Whatever the reason, after this they entered a golden era. For the next twelve years they were together. "Oolah was my longest and most successful relationship with anyone," said Rebecca. "I'll always be grateful for her love."

## *Don't Mess With Mr. Mao*

If you were to ask Mr. Mao (rhymes with
"pow"), he'd probably tell you he's just one of
the kids in a family of four children. Ever since
he was a kindhearted kitten, he's taken it upon
himself to be the guardian of his human siblings.

Mr. Mao was one of two kittens left from
an unplanned litter. When Donna arrived on
the scene to pick out a cat for her household,
she first selected the gray and black tabby who
resembled her childhood pet. But a neighbor girl
insisted she'd already chosen that one. So Donna
stared at the unassuming ginger-striped cat, who
seemed unaffected that he was the last one left.

He was no tabby, but Donna couldn't leave
without a new kitten, having promised one to
her two daughters. She decided to take a chance
on this little guy who squeaked as she held
him. Because he reminded her of a tiger, her
older daughter wanted to name him "something
Asian". Donna convinced her that "Mao"

sounded rather Asian, and was also a clever pun on the sound a cat makes.

Mr. Mao fit right in with their family. As he grew, he took on the responsibility of protecting the home and family from strangers of any species, and to welcome family friends as his own. Mr. Mao was always friendly with neighbors and house guests, but clearly did not approve of carpet cleaning people, was highly suspicious of repairmen, and sometimes hissed at delivery men.

Neighborhood cats learned quickly that Mr. Mao was intolerant of trespassers, and he communicated this to them clearly using any force necessary.

Donna jokes that Mr. Mao's father must have been a Bengal tiger. For more than half his life, Mao has weighed in at over twenty pounds and hunts like the king of his jungle. He regularly surveys his kingdom from the top of his personal rock in the garden or the redwood play-set tower in the backyard.

When a family member is ill or sad, Mr. Mao considers his post to be at their bedside. He stands watch, keeping a faithful vigil for anyone recovering from a range of maladies: stomach flu to minor surgeries, skinned knees to just plain bad days. And when he's sick, he lets Donna know in no uncertain terms, so she and the kids take turns standing vigil for him, too.

Mr. Mao has been a cat guardian for all four girls, but especially the two new babies. He kept a respectful distance from them as newborns but gradually warmed up to them as they grew older. Mr. Mao is patient with little people who don't understand that he, as a cat, has feelings, too. He good-naturedly accepts that toddlers do not realize that tails, long whiskers, and ears aren't for grabbing and pulling.

Mr. Mao's two big sisters play guitar for him; (he prefers acoustic, classical instrumentations.) Sometimes he even endures the humiliating ritual of a bath at the girls' hands. After they swaddle him in a beach towel and release him, it leaves him feeling exposed and vulnerable to any passing foes—not to mention embarrassed by how much less intimidating he appears when wet.

Mr. Mao is completely devoted to his family. Daily, he shows love, compassion, and a longing to protect his sisters—just like any other big brother.

## A Rough Beginning

When Alzheimer's disease necessitated Martha's move to a care center, her friends didn't know what to do with her cat Louie. Martha's family and friends already had pets. Since Louie was fearful of strangers, friends were reluctant to take him to a shelter.

Enter Alice, one of Martha's nurses, who agreed to adopt Louie. But, he wasn't happy about this and let Alice know it. Whenever she tried to pet Louie, he would nip at her as if to say "I'm warning you…leave me alone".

Alice wondered if she'd made a mistake. Perhaps Louie was grieving the loss of Martha.

One day, several weeks later, Alice was talking on the phone, elbows propped on the counter. She'd been chatting for a while when she sensed a presence. She held very still as Louie inched towards her, then rubbed his head contentedly against hers. She'd been accepted!

Years later, Louie and Alice are best buds. "I love him to pieces", she says, "and he finally loves me back." Sometimes the best friendships don't always start out smoothly.

ENJOY EACH DAY,
KNOWING HOW MUCH YOU'RE
LOVED AND ADMIRED...
AT LEAST BY YOUR CAT.

# What's in a Name?

In the Bible, Adam had the daunting task of naming all the animals in Creation. Do the names we give our feline friends tell more about us or the cats?

As a math teacher, Wanda always loved working with numbers and even though she's retired now, she still works with them. But now it's counting cats. She volunteers regularly at her local animal shelter and often ends up taking home the "difficult to adopt" cats.

Friends call her whenever a stray appears. Wanda the Cat Whisperer patiently coaxes abandoned cats out from under cars or out of trees. She takes the orphan to the vet for vaccinations and neutering/spaying, then finds a home for the little one, unless the kitty adopts her first. Presently eight felines have adopted her, so she's become very creative in naming them.

Sometimes strays appear on her deck chairs, as did the handsome black short hair with green eyes. En route home from the vet, he was "talking" so loudly (probably not thrilled about being neutered) that he earned the name, Yakety-Yak-Yak.

And Roswell? Wanda was wearing her Roswell, New Mexico (home of the alleged UFO incident) t-shirt when she found a kitten coated in fleas, on her stairway. After a bath, he looked like an alien, so Roswell just fit.

Wanda's cat with the distinctive markings started out with the name T.S. for Tiger Stripe, which morphed into T.S. Eliot, which became just Eliot. As a literary cat, Eliot enjoys sitting on the latest novel, usually while Wanda is trying to read it.

Wee Willie is, of course, a skinny little guy. And Wild Thing is well, a wild thing. FeFi has a Funky Ear, the "Fe" portion of FeFi. Initials work well for names, such as M.C. for Mama Cat and C.C. for Calico Cat.

Hmmm…what do you think the cats call Wanda?

## Hitching a Ride

Rob pulled into the parking lot at work, but when he got out of his truck, he heard mewing. It took him a couple of minutes to realize the kitten's cries were coming from the engine of his truck. He popped open the hood and there sat a frightened black kitten.

Rob recognized the little cat as belonging to his neighbor, the one who seemed to neglect his pets. Many times the kitten had shown up hungry at Rob's door, so he'd fed her. This feisty feline had survived on the truck engine for a 30-minute commute from Rob's home in the suburbs to his office downtown. Rob presumed this little one must have desperately wanted to flee her bad circumstances if she would hitch-hike on a truck engine just to escape.

Rob took the scared creature into the company office where everyone fussed over the sweet kitty who had survived such a long trek—under the hood of a moving vehicle.

Rob had to go on his service calls, so he left the kitten in the office. Later that afternoon, he returned to discover the office employees had pooled their funds and bought cat food, treats, a litter box and a soft bed. The little traveler was not going back; she was here to stay.

Fortunately Aaron, the company owner, was fine with the new resident. Actually, Aaron's wife had been hinting about getting a cat. So the next day, Aaron took the kitten home.

His wife, Debby, was totally taken with this traveling wonder and named the little black beauty "Sally Noir," which translates from French as "Black Sally." After a trip to the vet for a check-up and vaccinations, Sally Noir settled comfortably into Debby's and Aaron's posh high-rise apartment. Now Sally Noir shares their lives and their laps.

She happily greets Aaron at the door after work and jumps on him when he sits down. She then starts her ritual of putting her paws on either side of his face and licking his chin. Aaron's face lights up as Sally dissolves any tension.

Sally Noir completely charms Debby and Aaron. They feel Sally's unconditional love and acceptance, and her antics make them laugh. If Sally appears to be in a pensive mood, they speculate about what she is thinking, like: "Look at my humans—aren't they cute? And they're so tall!"

Sally Noir is also welcome at Aaron's office, where she has a second bed and the employees dote on her. Rob's neighbor never missed the cat who hitched a ride for a second chance at life.

Debby says that whenever she pets Sally Noir, she feels everything is right in her part of the world; all is calm. From this faithful feline she's learned that extraordinary happiness can be found in ordinary moments.

## *Do (Do) Unto Others*

As young children, we're taught the "Golden Rule," of treating others the way we would like to be treated. Maybe that doesn't pertain just to us humans.

Bach was a lovable, gray cat who'd been abandoned by a college student and left in an apartment. Fortunately Missy moved in, inheriting Bach, who now would have regular meals and loving care. But he always acted as though any meal might be his last and, understandably, had a great fear of being abandoned.

So Missy, and later her husband Matthew, always made Bach feel he was the most important creature in the room. When company would come over, Bach was the center of attention and was always lavishly fed!

But when Missy's mother-in-law came to visit for a couple weeks, she didn't fuss over Bach at all. Edith was a "dog person" and simply did not like cats. So she'd either ignore Bach completely or shake her finger at him when he did something innocent, like lounging on her bed.

After a week of Edith's aloofness, Bach took matters into his own paws. Edith's suitcase was open on the bedroom floor, so Bach decided to climb right into it and leave his own personal "calling card," making sure Edith would notice and remember him.

Missy was so embarrassed; fortunately, Edith thought it was hilarious. Edith suddenly realized that she had been treating Bach—and perhaps even her daughter-in-law—in a disrespectful manner and not at all the way she, herself, would want to be treated.

Now when Edith visits, she is attentive and kind to her daughter-in-law and makes sure to talk to Bach, pet him, and fuss over him. Who knew that a cat could so effectively teach the Golden Rule? (And Edith always closes her suitcase now.)

# *Patience*

Don't you wish we could go to the store to buy patience by the gallon, much the same way we buy milk? And wouldn't it be great never to run out of it when we need it most? We should take our cues from cats who wait patiently for a mouse to appear or for a pat on the head. A shy kitten named Coco taught Kate something about patience.

Kate adopted her kitty from a woman who had a habit of giving all the kittens in a litter the same name: Chanel. To differentiate, she gave them numbers, as in Chanel No. 1, No. 2, and of course Chanel No. 5. So Kate dubbed her new kitten "Coco" the nickname of the famous French designer, Gabrielle Chanel.

Once home, the borderline-feral kitten refused to come out from under the sofa in the basement. Kate's husband put the sofa on blocks so Coco could more easily be seen and fed.

But Coco wouldn't let anyone near her for about a month, when she finally let Kate touch her as she stretched out her hand with food.

After two months, she let Kate pet her, but not for very long before scampering back under the sofa. Coco, more hostile hermit than friendly feline, persisted in hiding in the basement.

But Kate continued patiently going downstairs every day to spend time with her. Coco eventually permitted Kate to pet her for longer and longer periods of time, finally allowing Kate to hold her.

After over five months in the basement, Coco ventured out from under the sofa and up the basement steps. She found a whole new world awaiting her upstairs.

Coco, in her own shy way, shows how patience has its rewards. If we pause and serenely look about our surroundings, solutions may appear, perspectives can shift, and eventually happiness will quietly come.

NEVER UNDERESTIMATE
   THE VALUE OF DOING NOTHING.

## Picture Perfect Pussycats

When Maria adopted Max and Trudy, she
had no idea that both tabby cats would one day
appear on greeting cards. Maria only knew that
she wanted to adopt a brother-sister duo, and
these two seemed perfect for her.

Maria is a designer at a small greeting card
company. So when the photographer there asked
if anyone in the office had photogenic cats,
Maria showed her pictures of Max and Trudy.
The photographer was impressed and set up a
time for the cats' photo shoot.

A week later, the photographer showed up at
Maria's home with all of her equipment to digitally
capture Max and Trudy. This photo session was
for capturing images that would be appropriate
for Easter.

The plan was for each cat to be placed in an
Easter basket; unfortunately, Max was too big
to fit in either one. Even without the eggs in it,

there was not enough room for stocky Max. But his petite sister Trudy was the perfect size, so she patiently posed in the basket, alongside colored eggs and a stuffed bunny. The result was an adorable Easter card.

The next month the photographer returned, hoping to get cat pictures for wedding anniversary cards. The scene was to be of Max and Trudy on Maria's bed. This had disaster written all over it.

The photographer brought in fragrant roses and fancy satin sheets and set up special lighting effects. Once everything was meticulously pre-pared and staged, Trudy got spooked and ran off to hide; Max played in the sheets and wouldn't show his face.

Since that hadn't worked, the frustrated photographer arranged several small, heart-shaped pillows on a chair in the bedroom. Max was placed next to them and immediately reached for one of the heart-shaped pillows. Voila… the perfect picture for an anniversary card. (Trudy never did come out of hiding the rest of the day; besides, she really prefers Easter with the baskets, eggs and soft, stuffed bunnies.)

A couple months later, the photographer returned again to take pictures of Max and Trudy. No pesky baskets or bed sheets this time. Max could clown around as much as he wanted since these pictures were going to be used on humorous birthday cards. The photographer sometimes used a feather on a stick to keep their attention, but for the majority of the time, the cats cooperated by posing in charming and amusing ways.

After the pictures were digitally enhanced on the computer, Trudy and Max were both wearing clothes, and on one card Max appeared to be driving a car.

Now Trudy and Max are known by name at the company. Maria even brought them into the office one day so everyone there could meet the now-famous felines.

Maria is happy to report that all of this fame has not gone to her cats' heads. They are still the loveable and entertaining creatures she adopted four years ago, but now she can wish friends "Happy Easter" or "Happy Birthday" with greeting cards featuring her photogenic felines.

# Purr-fect Justice

Amour, a loving black and white cat, had unique markings—a solid black heart just above her left rear leg. Jenna was studying French in school, so she named her cat "Amour," which means "love."

But there was no love lost between Amour and Bosco, the other cat in the house. Jenna's Dad, Jim, was concerned since Amour and his tortie Bosco absolutely did not get along. So Jim resorted to something that was really out of character for him.

While his teenage daughter Jenna was at school, Jim took Amour to the animal shelter. He explained the situation of Amour fighting with his cat and hoped they could find a good home for her.

When Jenna returned home, she searched everywhere for Amour. Jim fibbed and told her he'd seen Amour escape through an open basement window, and he just couldn't catch her.

Jenna was heartbroken. Jim, feeling guilty, helped Jenna put up "Lost Cat" signs throughout the neighborhood. Jenna didn't give up; she continued her search for Amour.

A few weeks later she and a girlfriend were browsing the pet store on a Friday, the day the local shelter showcases some of their cats and dogs, hoping they will be adopted. Jenna noticed a black and white cat that looked strangely familiar. She asked to hold this one and observed the black heart on her haunches. This was her long-lost cat!

By now Amour recognized Jenna and was purring and licking her hand. Jenna surmised that some kind-hearted person had found her lost cat and taken her to the shelter. She told the clerk at the pet store to "reserve this cat" for her and she'd be back with the adoption fees.

Jenna rushed home to tell her Dad the great news. Jim could hardly believe that Jenna and Amour had been reunited. He sheepishly returned to the pet store to pay the $100 adoption fee that covers vaccinations and spaying. Amour's time at the shelter must have mellowed her because she and Bosco soon would be on friendly terms.

Jim never has told Jenna the truth, but he has paid dearly for his deception. Remorseful, Jim dutifully cleans out Amour's litter box and buys her favorite food. Amour is not sure that she wants to forgive Jim and sometimes deposits a hairball or two on his bed. Purr-fect justice.

TOUGH TIMES
DON'T LAST FOREVER...
BUT GOD'S LOVE DOES.

# Extending the Paw of Friendship

Snickerdoodle, a tortie blend, could win the title of Miss Congeniality in a cat beauty pageant. Even when living at the animal shelter, she was friendly and outgoing to every cat or person she encountered.

Snickerdoodle, whose name evolved into "Doodlebug" and eventually just "Bug," became part of Allison's and Isaac's household as a four-month-old kitten. The young couple wanted a "sibling" for their cat Taffy. When they were at the shelter, the cordial kitten reached out a paw and tapped Allison as she passed. Suddenly, Bug had a new home.

Within one week of being introduced to Taffy, Bug was cuddling with her like a loving sibling. Now if curious Taffy accidentally gets shut in a closet, Bug stubbornly sits in front of the door, refusing to move and meowing as if to say, "My sister is in here! Please open!"

Always affectionate, Bug perches on Isaac's shoulder and rubs up against his ear. On trips to the vet, this congenial cat tries to make friends, even with the dogs.

Allison and Isaac foster cats, so they might host as many as three litter mates at one time. While they're at work, they keep any feline guests in their large extra bedroom. Bug stretches a front leg under the closed bedroom door, extending her paw of friendship. It's her way of "shaking paws" to welcome the fostered cats.

Sometimes amiable Bug pushes a flattened cloth mouse under the door to amuse the visitors. When the foster cats come out of the bedroom, she continues her hospitality by giving each guest a complimentary bath with her tongue.

She's the peacekeeper, the diplomat between Taffy and any other cats. Bug's gregarious nature is contagious; she wins over even a seemingly unsociable cat. She freely shares her playthings, a soft quilt, or a spot in the sun. Genuinely kind to everyone—both cats and humans—Bug is always ready to extend her paw of friendship.

## Cat Nanny

A beautiful tortoiseshell cat appeared on the Spencers' doorstep one day. They named her Maggie, and it was as though she'd been sent to help shape up the family, sort of like a British nanny.

Smart and resourceful, Maggie knew that a loud smack on the blinds would awaken most of the family members in the morning. None of this sleeping in; this cat ran a tight ship.

Maggie tried to keep the family on some sort of timetable. On rare occasions when the mother, Leslie, would feed Maggie a little late, she would jump up on top of the refrigerator right next to the box of cat food and meow loudly as if to say, "Can we stay on schedule here? It's time to eat!"

They called Maggie a "social eater" because she would fetch any available family members and lead them into the kitchen before she'd start eating. Maggie was merely teaching them the joys of dining together as a family.

Maggie seemed more human than cat-like in her taste. She loved the sound of the human voice, so whenever Leslie would read to her young children, Maggie would show up and get on the back of the couch and listen. If Leslie would listen to books on CD, Maggie would come out of wherever she was napping to listen.

Maggie enjoyed watching cat food commercials on television. She'd stop whatever she was doing to stare intently. A favorite place to perch was on the cable box. Maggie was quite the "TV critic" and was known to throw up on the cable box if she didn't like a certain show. The Spencers went through several cable boxes.

Just like a nanny, Maggie helped with behavioral problems. Their five year old son Patrick had some anger issues, so they were trying to modify his behavior using the technique of time-out. They had a "time-out chair" and used a timer to set the limits. The rule was if Patrick got up before the timer went off, he had to sit there for another minute.

One day Patrick was having a bad day and would not cooperate at all. He was put in the time-out chair, where he was crying and throwing a tantrum.

Maggie came out of her hiding place and jumped up on Patrick's lap. He pushed her off and she jumped back up. It happened a few more times and then she nipped him. It surprised Patrick so much that he stopped crying and let Maggie come back on his lap. He stroked her gently and she soothed his little hyperactive soul. The calming power of a cat was all in a day's work for Maggie.

IF YOU OWN A KITTEN,
LIFE OVERFLOWS
        WITH CUTENESS.

## Cats on the Keys

If Marilyn hears her piano suddenly start to play in the middle of the night, she knows it's either Rex or Roi walking along the keys. Her two slender gray cats enjoy playing their own compositions. Their melodies usually have a rather contemporary, dissonant sound, but she considers it music, nonetheless.

Marilyn teaches piano lessons in her home to students who range in age from seven to seventeen, so Rex and Roi are accustomed to hearing a variety of strange sounds emanating from her music studio.

While waiting for a lesson to begin, the students enjoy playing with either Rex or Roi. The playful cats are happy to distract students who may be nervous about their upcoming lessons, especially if they have not practiced enough that week.

Rex and Roi know how to work the room. Once a lesson begins, one cat will jump on the piano bench and quietly sit beside the student as she plays her scales, while the other cat entertains the student's mother across the room.

Sometimes after a good lesson, Marilyn will allow her musical scholars to place the cat's paws on the piano to help play another song. Marilyn joins in so there are four hands and two paws on the keyboard. Rex and Roi enjoy showcasing their musical talents and the kids think it's fun. Who wouldn't enjoy a good piano duet with a cat?

When the students are ready to return home, Marilyn hands them a sticky roller so they can remove the cat hair from their clothes. She doesn't want the parents to think their child's lessons consist of playing only with cats instead of the piano.

But often Marilyn does wonder: do the students come for her teaching expertise or to play with her amazing cats? It's probably a little of both.

# A Tale of Two Kitties

It was the best of times, it was the worst of times, it was a time in Lola's life when two little kitties made all the difference.

Tobias, Toby for short, was a rowdy and loving orange tabby Lola had adopted from a shelter. Shortly after acquiring Toby, she inherited Pockets, a beautiful Siamese. Lola's father had deposited the cat with her when he left for a European vacation, then neglected to pick him up when he returned.

The two toms fought for about three weeks, but then must have reached a truce because after that they were best buddies for the next 20 years.

Toby's hobby was to climb the curtains, then shred them as he slid down. He managed to pull his claws all across her sofa so that, too, was shredded. But Lola loved Toby so much that she didn't really care that her furniture and drapes had been reduced to strings.

Lola lived in a third floor apartment at the time and when Toby would hear her coming up the steps, he'd leap toward her and grab onto her with his claws. Lola had several scratches, "badges of honor" as she preferred to call them.

Lola was single at the time and felt that Toby was like a partner to her…he'd look deep into her eyes and they seemed to be on the same wavelength. Toby even slept in her arms. Pockets would give Lola "love bites," at least that's what she'd call it when he'd affectionately nip at her nose.

Both Toby and Pockets traveled back and forth across the country with Lola more than once as she changed jobs. The traveling cats saga began many years ago when one summer, Lola drove with a girlfriend and the two cats in an un-air-conditioned car from Minnesota to Idaho for a new job there.

A few years later, Lola had to move to Rhode Island for a different job. On Thanksgiving Day, the busiest day for the airlines, she flew with her two cats to the East coast. They changed planes in Chicago, landing eventually in Boston. Throughout all this, Lola was wrangling two cat carriers plus luggage. By the time she reached the car rental, she was in tears. The cats were meowing in empathy. It was love for her cats—and determination—that got her through.

Two years later, Lola suffered a back injury while visiting the Twin Cities and ended up staying there. The cats had to be flown back from Rhode Island to Minneapolis by her friends. By now these cats deserved "frequent flyer miles" for the plane trips they'd endured.

Lola needed to be on bed rest for her back injury, so both cats comforted her. Toby was especially attentive as he'd sit on her chest and look directly into her eyes as if to say, "How are you doing today? I'm going to care for you." Then he'd start to knead her as though he were her personal feline chiropractor.

Lola recovered from her injuries, feeling that the unconditional, ongoing love from her cats hastened her healing. She started her own business in Minneapolis; Pockets and Toby were grateful to stay in one city. For felines or their human friends, it's always more fun to travel life's roads with someone you love.

## Trendy Kitty

For weeks, Miranda had been wishing, begging, and praying for a kitten. But her family had several dogs, so getting a cat seemed impossible…until one day in June.

Her mother, Rhonda, had taken Miranda and several friends on a picnic in the country. While there, they spotted some abandoned kittens. Miranda, a kind-hearted ten-year-old, worried about their welfare. She refused to leave until she could rescue these felines. So Miranda and her friends managed to catch them. The trip home in the van was noisy, with kittens meowing and kids laughing and squealing with delight. After calling their parents to get permission, Miranda's friends each got to take home a kitty.

Miranda named her gray tabby "Angel" since she thought her kitty might have been heaven-sent. The newcomer adjusted quickly to a household of dogs. Angel acted angelic around Rhonda and Miranda, but her devilish side came out when the canines appeared.

Angel would sit on a bar stool in the kitchen and wait for one of the dogs to walk by. Whack! She'd swat one of them on the nose and send him yelping. The dogs soon learned that Angel was anything but one.

Miranda, a fashion diva even at ten, enjoyed dressing up Angel. She put her in doll clothes and cradled her like a baby. Angel was an incredibly patient cat, even permitting Miranda to wheel her around the house in a baby buggy. If Miranda couldn't locate Angel, sometimes she'd discover her asleep in the doll bed.

Now, seven years later, Angel is still Miranda's beloved cat and they share a bedroom. Miranda is a cheerleader at her high school, so now Angel sports a kitty cheerleader outfit. Angel actually seems to enjoy dressing up and has accumulated quite an impressive wardrobe over the years. Who knew a cat could be a fashionista?

## A Feline Mayberry

Otto did not intend to have a cat in his posh apartment, but fortunately for his health, he ended up with two of them.

His wife had planted the idea of adopting a cat, so when an employee at Otto's office brought in two rescued kittens, he took them home. Sheba and Sally became part of their family.

Several months later, Otto went in for his annual physical exam. The nurse took his blood pressure, which was high. Otto began talking about his cats, Sally and Sheba, as he tends to do. When the nurse finished other tests, she took Otto's blood pressure again. His second reading was much lower; the nurse believed it was due to Otto becoming calmer as he talked about his cats.

Otto convinced his friend Bruno, who lives in Otto's native country of Germany, that getting a cat would be good for his health. Bruno is now a confirmed cat lover and when they talk on the phone, he answers with, "Hello Meow," and ends with "Goodbye Meow." (Both men now have great blood pressure.)

MOST PROBLEMS CAN BE LICKED
WITH A POSITIVE ATTITUDE.

# The Magnificat

If man could be crossed with the cat it would improve man, but it would deteriorate the cat.
—Mark Twain, 1894

Cats are advanced creatures. They've always acted more civilized than we humans. And cats in Italy certainly live la dolce vita.

David and Cynthia had joined a walking tour of Rome. Their guide Lucia paused in front of the Roman square, Largo di Torre Argentina, site of four ancient temples. "Here," she announced, "is where Emperor Julius Caesar was assassinated in 44 B.C."

They looked around at the glorious ancient temple ruins…with cats draped over them! Felines of all colors and breeds were roaming freely through the ruins; some resting dramatically on the stumps of Roman columns.

"These are the gatti di Roma, the cats of Rome," Lucia proclaimed. "And Rome is ruled by cats!" She added that the site of Caesar's demise is now the largest cat sanctuary in Rome, where cats find shelter from the traffic of the city.

"Sometimes," laughed Lucia, "the tourists are more interested in the cats than the ruins!"

According to the guide, the cats are provided with food and shelter, mainly by an international group of volunteers who raise funds for them also to be spayed or neutered and vaccinated. It's not unusual for tourists to contribute to the fund. Here, too, is an underground no-kill shelter where cats with disabilities reside, plus an area housing those up for adoption.

Several cats also preside at the ruins of the famous Coliseum. Here gladiators lost their lives in gruesome ways and torture was a sport. Both the square at Torre Argentina and the Coliseum were sites of violent acts of man's inhumanity to man.

What a contrast with the tranquil felines who, except for a rare scuffle, are living peacefully together. Wonder why mere humans are in charge of the planet?

## The Chosen Few

Through the years, several cats have meandered in and out of Ann's life. "Anyone can have a dog," says Ann, "but a cat chooses you. You get a special feeling from a cat, a real connection to nature. You're chosen."

Presently she and her family have been chosen by three felines—Tambini, Snow, and Buttons—who always keep life interesting.

Tambini, a Russian blue mix adopted from a shelter, appreciates the charming 100-year-old home that Ann and her husband Brian renovated in a Chicago suburb. Tambini enjoys exploring the unfinished area of the basement, especially in autumn. When temperatures drop outside, mice and chipmunks seek warmth and refuge there. How kind of the family to arrange for Tambini's hunting expeditions at his private rodent refuge in the basement.

One October, a chipmunk escaped from the basement, ran all the way to the top floor and into a guest bedroom. Brian was certain that Tambini the Hunter would dispense with this chipmunk for them, so he put the cat in the bedroom and closed the door.

Evidently, both creatures had been frightened by all the confusion. So when Brian opened the door again, the cat and the chipmunk sat side-by-side under the bed, staring back at him with wide eyes as if to say, "Not our idea!"

Brian finally trapped the chipmunk under a bowl and set him loose outside. Tambini later emerged from under the bed, seeming a bit embarrassed by the whole incident.

Then there's Buttons, the gray and white cat with a bob tail, who is always first to initiate the annual winter ritual: the Climbing of the

Christmas Tree. One December morning, Buttons scrambled all the way to the top of the beautifully-decorated evergreen. It swayed back and forth while Ann held her breath, hoping the kitty would climb down without hurting himself. Fortunately, both the tree and Buttons survived the adventure.

Later Buttons brought Ann some ornaments as though he were offering to help Ann redecorate. The next evening, Ann found all three cats nestled among the gifts under the illuminated tree, like three feline magi.

Snow, their black cat with a white collar, finds his favorite place next to Ann in their king-sized bed. Extremely possessive of Ann, Snow doesn't appreciate sharing the bed with Paco, their pug dog. When Paco snoozes, he snores loudly. This startles Snow, who gives him a hard whack on the nose then chases him around the bed, with Paco eventually hiding in the pillows. It's amazing that Ann and Brian get any sleep at all.

Some evenings there's what Ann calls the "Nighttime Romp." All three cats decide to chase each other–or the dog–through the house, up and down the stairs.

Ann and her family enjoy the cats' antics as well as their often peaceful presence. "One of the things I love about our cats is they create a tranquil environment. They find the warmest spot in the room, even with just a glimmer of sunlight, and rest there. Cats seem to exude serenity and harmony." Spoken by a true cat-lover whose nights are not always silent ones.

# Power Napping

Watching a cat sleep is one of the best natural tranquilizers. Cats will relax every muscle and drape themselves over a chair or sometimes languorously stretch out on a bed. Other times they curl up in a ball and sleep roundly and soundly.

Sovereigns of slumber, cats are nap experts. It's no coincidence that a type of sleeping was named in their honor: the cat nap. You never hear, "Oh, I think I'll take a quick dog nap or a hamster nap." That's because when it comes to napping, cats are the professionals.

Europeans imitate them by taking afternoon siestas, enjoying a leisurely lunch and ensuing nap. But for most sleep-deprived Americans, naps are rare and lunch often means gulping down a sandwich while multi-tasking. Cats find such uncivilized behavior appalling.

We could learn from the wise cat who lives in the present, doesn't stress about the past, or worry about the future. And cats know that life always looks better after a nap. Sweet dreams!

# LIFE ALWAYS LOOKS BETTER
## AFTER A GOOD NAP.

# Curiosity

Sometimes the stress of the world overtakes us and we perform daily chores on autopilot as we speed through life. Laurie had been going full tilt when her inquisitive Siamese cat, Sheba, taught her a lesson about slowing down.

It was a typical busy Saturday morning and Laurie was doing laundry. She had a load of jeans in the dryer when she realized she needed to get groceries. So she opened the dryer door as a way of turning if off. After a bit, she decided she really didn't want to get out in the rain for the few items she had on her list, so she closed the dryer door and started cleaning house. What Laurie did not realize is that Sheba had climbed into the open dryer to find a nice, warm, place for a nap on a cold, rainy day.

It never occurred to Laurie to look inside the dryer before shutting the door a second time. When the dryer started up again, it sounded awfully loud but Laurie decided it was just the heavy jeans making the noise. Fortunately for Sheba's sake, after about 5 minutes, Laurie discovered she needed more groceries, so before leaving, she turned the dryer off by using the dial.

Then she heard a terrible noise coming from the dryer–and realized it was her cat's cry. She thought maybe Sheba had crawled behind the dryer and somehow gotten herself trapped that way…never dreaming she was actually in the dryer!

When she opened the dryer door, a very dizzy Sheba staggered out! She was so dizzy she could hardly walk and let out a yelp that sounded more like the howl of a wounded coyote.

Laurie was in tears and immediately called the vet, telling him she had accidentally dried her cat in the dryer. The vet advised her to keep Sheba calm and get her there as quickly as possible. Keep her calm? Laurie could barely keep herself calm—and she hadn't been whirling around in a dryer for five minutes! She phoned her parents, who lived nearby, to help her transport the rattled Sheba to the vet.

When they arrived at the doctor's office, he said that a few more minutes in the dryer and the cat's curiosity would have…well, killed her. Miraculously, Sheba had only a bruised tail and a bitten tongue. Her tail did eventually heal, but never would go entirely straight, even after the five minutes she'd spent on permanent press.

But from that day on, Laurie always would pause and take a second look inside the dryer before closing the door. Perhaps Sheba was preparing Laurie for parenthood since about a year after the dryer incident, Laurie and her husband Steve started their family with their son Mark.

Sheba went on to live happily for many more years. Laurie commented that several of Sheba's antics helped her "train" for being the mother of an inquisitive and exploring toddler.

Cats often teach us lessons that we need to learn. Laurie is such a good student—she always checks any appliance before turning it on. She never knows what curious creature might have just crawled inside.

# Another Word for "Cat"

An American couple was traveling in Paris and struck up a conversation with a Frenchman. Although the Frenchman spoke excellent English, he graciously humored the tourists by letting them try their fractured French.

"Avez-vous des enfants? (Do you have children?") the Frenchman inquired.

Now the American woman actually knew more Spanish than French but wanted to reply in French with "No, but we have a cat."

However, she was evidently still thinking of the Spanish word for "cat," which is "gato," and she blurted out a sort of Spanish-French combo using the correct French verb but the Spanish noun for cat. Unfortunately, the French noun sounds just like "gato," but means something completely different than "cat."

So in response to "Do you have any children?" She intended to reply, "No, but we have a cat." Instead the American proudly responded with, "Non, mais nous avons un gâteaux!" (No, but we have a cake!)

The Frenchman replied, "And you Americans think the French love their food."

REMEMBER...
    PLAY A LITTLE EVERY DAY.

# A Blessing on a Summer Day

A warm-hearted cat came into Bev's life during a blazing hot July in Kansas City. It all began when she noticed a colony of feral cats hanging around a construction site next to where she worked. Bev took pity on them and began leaving bowls of food and water near the site.

But one Thursday as she was getting ready to go home, she saw a flash of color out of the corner of her eye. It was a kitten. Limping and mewing desperately, the skin-and-bones kitty looked like she'd been in a fight. Bev surmised she'd been picked on by the cats from the construction area.

With over 100-degree temperatures predicted for the weekend, she knew the kitten probably wouldn't survive if she didn't help her.

So after work on Friday, armed with cat treats and food, Bev settled down to rescue the little creature. She had no sooner perched on a curb in the simmering heat when she realized she'd landed in someone's castoff chewing gum.

The kitten finally emerged, coming near Bev and then repeatedly running off. Bev had already named her "Blaze" since she'd appeared during a blazing hot summer and her coloring included the fiery colors of orange, gold, and reddish brown.

After two frustrating hours of "catch me if you can," Bev was about ready to give up. It was a sweltering July day, plus she was sitting in gum! As a last-ditch effort, Bev took a blanket from her car, threw it over Blaze and popped her in the carrier. She wondered why she hadn't thought of this solution two hours earlier. Once home, Blaze ate heartily, then retreated under the bed, coming out only occasionally during the weekend.

On Monday, Bev took Blaze to the vet where her leg was treated with antibiotics and when it had healed, she was eventually spayed. A few weeks later, one of Bev's co-workers, Natalie, adopted Blaze.

Unfortunately, after less than a week, Natalie returned to work with Blaze in the carrier, saying that she could not get her to come out from under the bed, and she simply refused to eat anything. Natalie knew this was not going to work out.

Bev often rescues and finds homes for cats, so she has a "cat-back guarantee." Of course, she agreed to take back Blaze. The minute Blaze saw Bev, she started purring. Perhaps Blaze had bonded so strongly with her rescuer that nobody else would do as her human companion. Whatever it was, Blaze was thrilled to be back with Bev.

Blaze loved her life with Bev. She'd sit on her lap, follow her everywhere, and try to be part of whatever she was doing. If she was eating, Blaze had to eat; if she was reading, Blaze sat on the newspaper; if she went to bed, Blaze followed.

Blaze had taken a risk in trusting Bev, just as Bev did by taking in this stray cat. But Bev understood that if you don't take chances, you could miss out on love, happiness, or other good things life may offer…including the blessings of a cat rescued on a hot summer day.

## A Catitude of Gratitude

The daily rains had made Spring that year a miserable one…at least for this cat. He was living in a storm sewer when Carolyn spotted him while out for her daily walk. The black and white feline was sitting in a couple inches of water, crying and complaining pitifully about his plight.

The beleaguered creature let Carolyn pet him and looked at her as though he were trying to tell his tale of abandonment. A nearby neighbor said that he'd been there about a week and that she'd left food for him, but could not get him to leave that spot, even in torrential rain.

For the next three days Carolyn checked on the dejected feline, who continued to cry. He was a good-sized cat; Carolyn guessed about 17 pounds. He allowed her to pet him and she noticed he only had half a tail. He needed to be rescued.

But Carolyn already had two cats that didn't really get along with each other, so how could she take in one more? Love trumped logic. She showed up with a cat carrier with food in it and shoved in the big guy.

He wailed en route to the vet, but once there, he seemed to calm down. After he was dried off, vaccinated, and groomed, he looked almost regal with his striking white markings. Carolyn named him Buster.

At home, Buster managed to make friends with Carolyn's other two cats, Inca and Max, who felt such animosity toward one another that she had to always keep them separated. Buster soon became the peacekeeper.

Buster seemed to know that Carolyn had rescued him from a harsh life on the street. To show his gratitude, almost daily Buster would bring Carolyn "civilized prey," namely socks, underwear, and once even her fleece jacket. One day Carolyn found seven "killed" socks in a pile, all little gifts of gratitude.

Buster does his best to comfort his human. Whenever Carolyn is sick, Buster tries to "cuddle away" the illness. He curls up next to her and purrs. Buster is completely devoted to Carolyn, and she is grateful for his unconditional love.

She adores Buster's remarkably positive attitude of gratitude. His "catitude" is a simple one: practice gratitude daily and life is much sunnier.

DEAR GOD,
THANK YOU FOR
SENDING A LOVING
HUMAN TO
RESCUE ME.

## Sweet Survivors

Some cats are extraordinary just because they are survivors. For over ten years, Pete and his wife have cared for a colony of feral cats that live beneath an abandoned riverboat wharf in Omaha.

When the compassionate couple first took on this mission, there were over 12 cats at the wharf, and the only person looking after them was a homeless guy named Jake. Although they never met Jake, Pete and Cassie communicated with him via notes on scrap paper.

Jake generously left the cats whatever food he could salvage—french fries, hamburgers, or pieces of bread. When he moved on, Pete and Cassie took up the cause.

But new cats kept showing up at the river and producing more and more cats. So over the years, Pete and Cassie arranged for all those they could catch to be spayed or neutered. The cat-loving couple has found homes for more than 15 cats and brought six into their home to join their three other felines.

When Pete captured Moe, he was a thrashing, frightened tom. Bunk, a scruffy red kitten, came out shyly to watch them, but after the first touch, he stuck to them like glue. Twice he followed Pete and Cassie back to their car, and they returned him to his mother. The third time they realized that Bunk had adopted them, so they let him ride in their backpack and took him home.

A week later they trapped and adopted his sister, Sissy, mainly so Bunk would have someone to pester besides them. They also rescued Mimsy and Mimi, another sibling pair. They finally managed to catch and have spayed their mother, a feisty feral they call Mad Mama.

Then there was Bunny, who appeared beneath the wharf one September day. They'd set out the cat food as usual and were getting ready to leave when a pack of kittens spilled out of a tunnel and scampered toward the chow. One in particular caught their attention—a tiny gray kitten who ran with an odd gait. Their niece Chloe was helping them distribute the food and exclaimed, "Something's wrong with that kitty!"

The kitten was obviously sick, with an infected eye sealed shut and a large abscess on her neck. Pete was able to pick her up while she was trying to eat. She was too sick to struggle as he put her in his backpack. When their vet at the

Cat Clinic told them that the procedure to save this sick little creature would cost over $500, Pete just shrugged and said, "Well, we can't let her die."

Bunny is now, according to the couple, the World's Cutest Cat and a total prima donna. Pete feels that people don't understand feral cats. Once adopted, these cats become fiercely loyal to the humans who saved them.

"True, they don't like strangers," comments Pete. "But as soon as our front door closes and interlopers are gone, these cats pour their attention and affection on their own little 'cat colony', which includes lucky wildcat humans like us."

## *Healing Hearts*

The light of Emily's life was extinguished when Josh died. The sudden death of her young husband left her devastated and barely able to go on. As if on auto-pilot, Emily daily tended to their cat Misty—feeding her, giving her fresh water, cleaning the litter box. That was about all Emily had the energy or desire to do. It seemed as if both Emily and her cat merely existed.

Misty had been especially close to Josh. She'd jump up on his lap when he was at the computer or watching TV. She'd follow him around when he came home from work. Within a month of Josh's unexpected passing, Misty ended up in the emergency vet center. She had stopped eating.

Consequently, her liver function test results were not good and her bodily functions were beginning to shut down. She spent four days in a feline intensive care unit where she finally began to stabilize, but none of the vets at the clinic could find a medical explanation for Misty's deteriorating health.

The staff was asking Emily about Misty's activities when Emily mentioned the recent loss of her husband. Then it dawned on her: could Misty be dying of a broken heart? Emily had read that it wasn't unusual for an animal to grieve the loss of another animal or a human with whom they'd been close.

But how could she help Misty mourn this loss and still regain her health? She took Misty home and hoped for a miracle to keep her eating. Emily's close friend Kate, who had never had a pet in her life, suggested she put some possession of Josh's on the floor for Misty. It was worth a try.

Emily chose Josh's bathrobe that she purposely had kept on the hook behind the bathroom door. Just looking at it helped Emily feel Josh's presence. Perhaps his scent or the look and feel of the robe might remind Misty of Josh. Since one of Misty's favorite places was under the bed, Emily placed Josh's robe there. Misty immediately snuggled up to it. Over the next few weeks, she slowly started eating, gaining weight and becoming more playful.

Emily had not recognized that while she was lost in her own grief, Misty had come close to dying from hers. When Misty had stopped eating and was generally shutting down, it was just what Emily had felt like doing, too. But Emily now understood she needed to shift her focus to Misty.

Emily now plays more with Misty and tries to give her enough love for two people. Both of them still miss Josh, but they are trying to rebuild their lives. To this day, Josh's robe remains under the bed, with Misty cuddling it for comfort whenever she needs it. Emily and Misty have traveled the lonely road of grief, but together they will find the path of healing.

## *Amazing Grace*

Grace appeared in Beth's life one summer. Every morning when she arrived at work, and every night when she left, Beth noticed a gray and white cat dodging around the parked cars on the rooftop lot. How could a cat survive on a seven-story building parking lot, especially in the summer?

Beth put out bowls of food and water and tried every day to capture the cat, but no luck. She finally enlisted the help of her husband, Adam, and they returned one night with a cat carrier. Eventually Adam managed to lure the cat with treats and she jumped into the carrier.

According to the vet, this frightened cat had been hit by a car, leaving it with only one good eye. By grace, she had survived the collision and then life on a rooftop parking lot. So Beth and Adam named her Amazing Grace…Grace for short.

Beth was very patient with the skittish Grace. It took nine months after the dramatic rescue for Grace to curl up beside Beth on her bed, then another three months for her to allow Beth to even touch her.

But when Grace finally did decide to trust Beth, it was a complete and consuming trust. She followed her human friend everywhere, always a loving presence.

When a divorce turned life upside down and left Beth feeling as though she wasn't worthy of much, Grace helped her to feel valued and needed. Now it was Grace doing the rescuing.

Grace made sure that Beth never came home to an empty house. The sweet cat was always there, waiting at the door when Beth came home and sleeping beside her at night. When Beth would sit down, Grace would jump on her lap, purring in the most comforting way. No longer shy, she'd nuzzle Beth or rub up against her legs, as if she knew extra care was needed.

Grace's complete faith in and devotion to Beth gave her a new purpose. Beth had helped this cat heal from a broken past. Now when her life felt broken, she was saved by Grace... an Amazing Grace.

# Cats Just Know

Cats just know. They intuitively recognize kind-hearted people and know where they live and work.

Cheryl would often find a stray cat next to her car when she left work to drive home. It happened so frequently that she began to wonder if in the back of her car window there was a sign, visible only to felines, that read: "Cat Lover on Board!"

Martin and Beverly think there may be a similar visible-only-to-cats sign hanging outside their home. Affectionately called Kitty Grandma and Kitty Grandpa by their grandchildren, they've had several cats just appear out of nowhere on their front steps.

They always feed them, care for them, and try to find homes if they are not able to adopt them at the time. They joke that word must have spread throughout the local animal population that this is the home of two confirmed cat lovers.

Cats are discerning judges of character. They know who will return their affections. Cats just know.

FILL YOUR LIFE WITH LOVE,
AND YOU WILL LOVE YOUR LIFE.